R o b o t
Coloring Book for Kids

This coloring book belongs to:

_____

My name is:

_____

Circle the letters in your name.
Underline the first letter.

a   b   c   d   e   f   g

h   i   j   k   l   m   n

o   p   q   r   s   t   u

v   w   x   y   z

Robots are machines that
are programmed to do
certain tasks.

The robots in this coloring
book are pretend.

COLOR

Color the robot to match the color words.

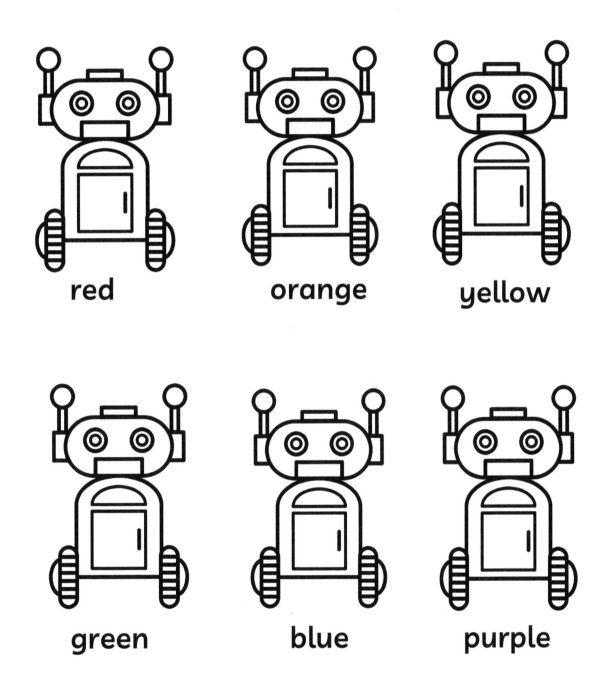

red

orange

yellow

green

blue

purple

The Robots

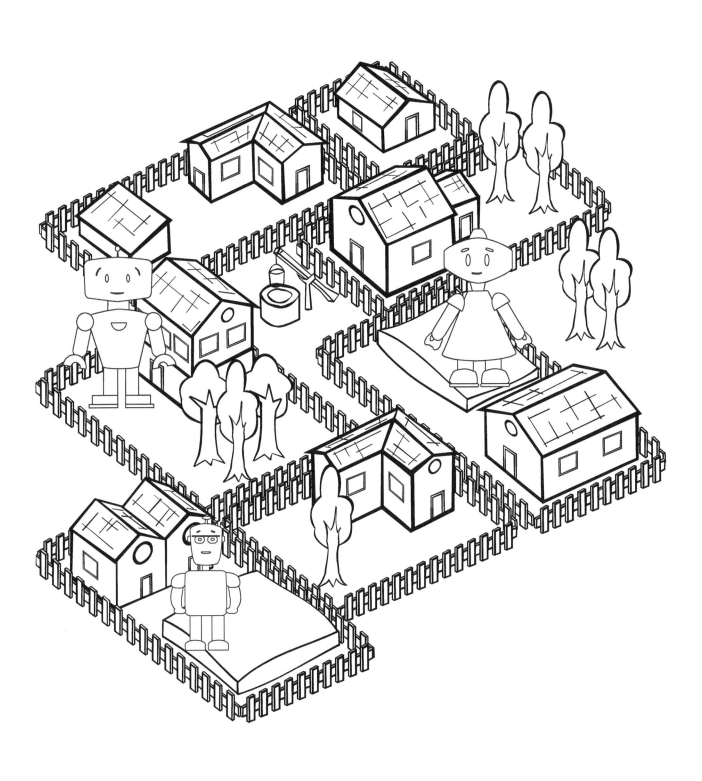

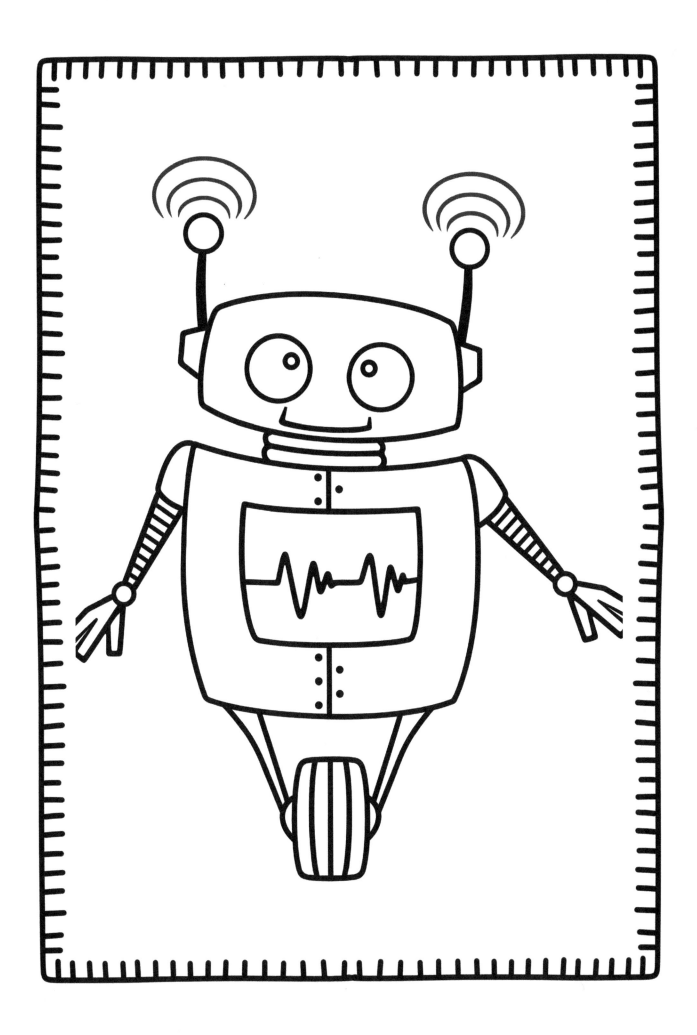

Trace & Color

Robot Land

City Robots

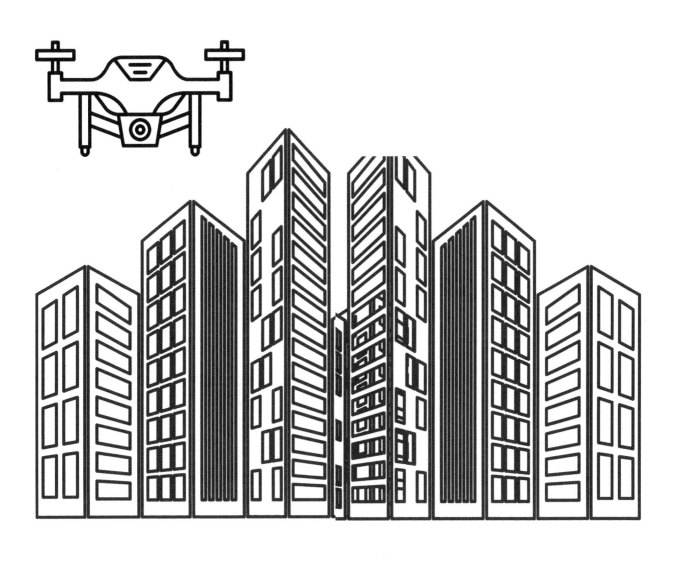

VACATION TIME

Road Trip

\

Trace

Trace the lines from left to right.

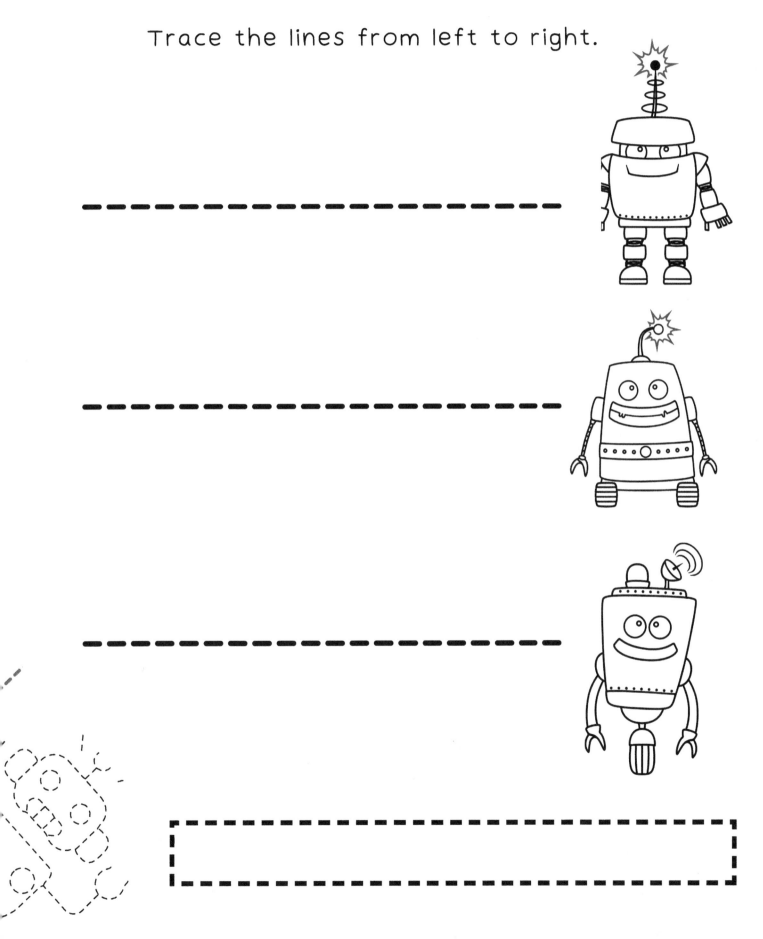

SPELL IT

Trace the letters of the alphabet for the word below.

ROBOT

A	B	C	D	E	F
G	H	I	J	K	L
M	N	O	P	Q	R
S	T	U	V	W	X
Y	Z				

SPELL IT

Trace the letters of the alphabet for the word below.

C O D E

A	B	C	D	E	F
G	H	I	J	K	L
M	N	O	P	Q	R
S	T	U	V	W	X
Y	Z				

Trace

Trace and color in the shapes below.

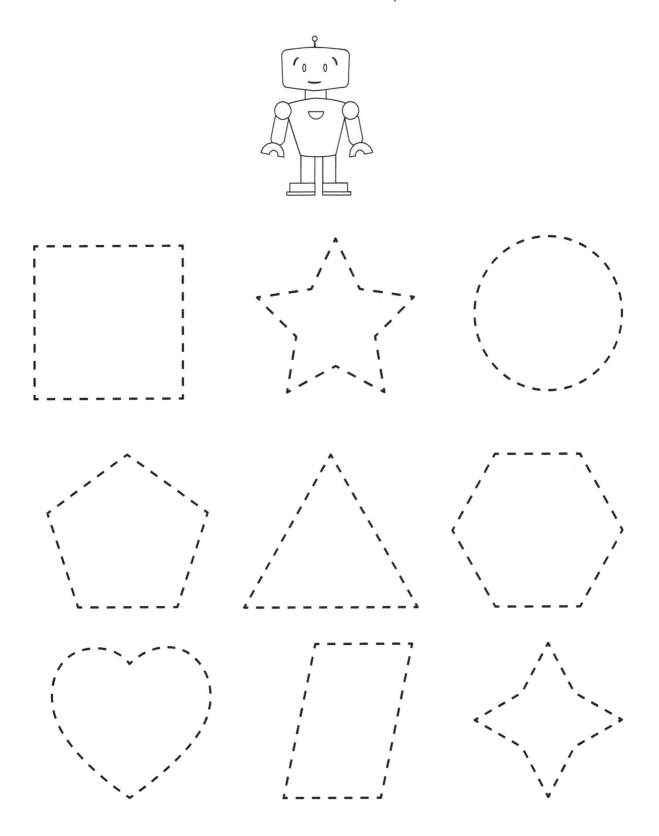

Trace

Trace & Color

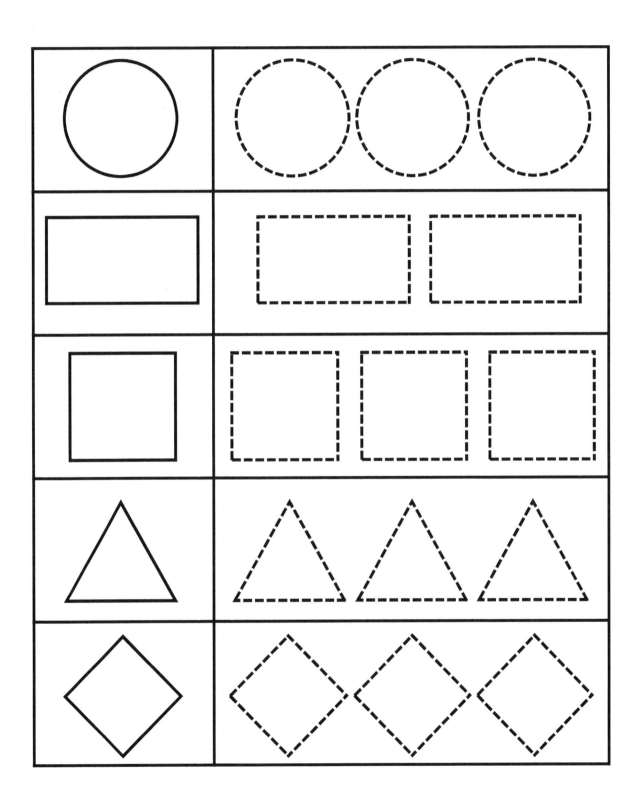

Color the Circles

Color the circles yellow.

Color the Squares

Color the squares red.

Robot Scramble

Follow the paths to find the owner of the robot.

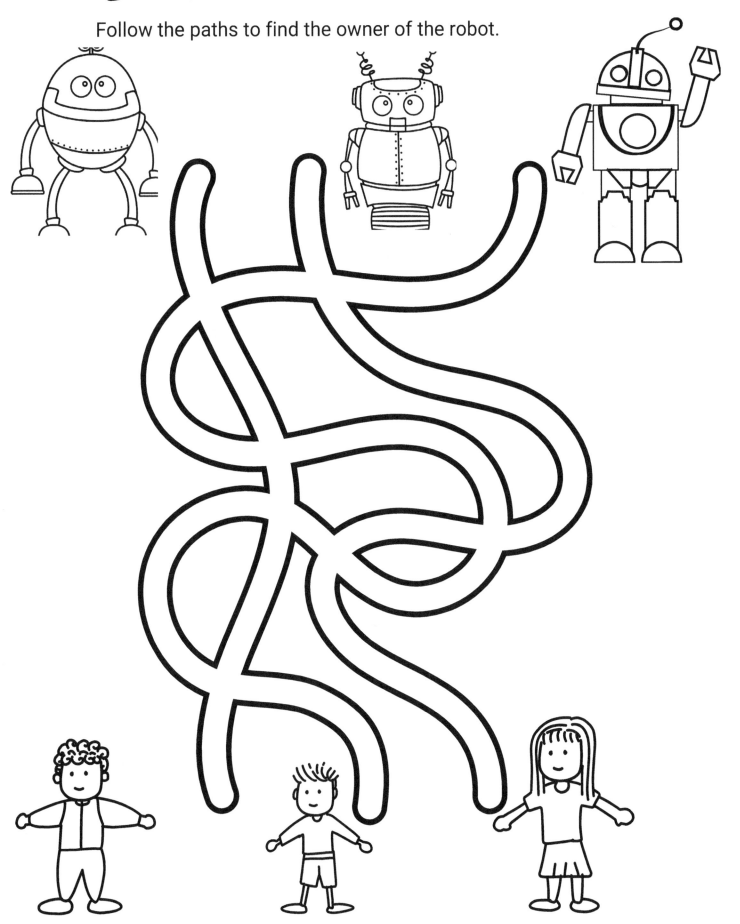

Robot Numbers

Color the numbers

Number Trace

Number Trace

6   6   6   6

7   7   7   7

8   8   8   8

9   9   9   9

10   10   10   10

iMystery - Shapes

Count all the shapes and write the numbers below

Build a Robot

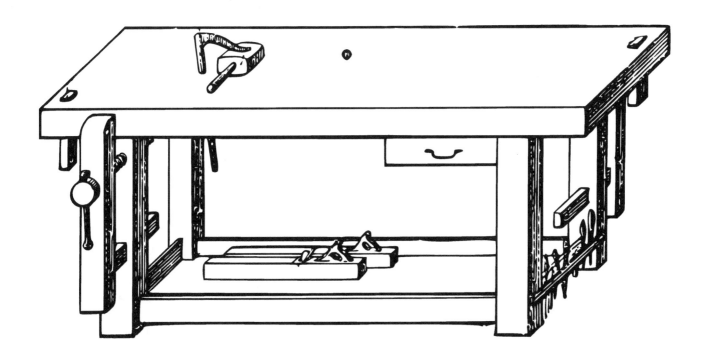

Build a robot

Robot Friends